My Prayer Journal

3 Month Bible Study & Worship Guide For the Creative Soul

NL PUBLISHING

All Contents Copyright © 2020 Naudia Lorraine

All Rights Reserved. No part of this document or accompanying files may be reproduced or transmitted in any form, electronic or otherwise, by any means without the prior written permission of the publisher, except by reviewers who may quote brief passages in a review.

ISBN: 978-1-7339531-2-2

For permission requests, please email
support@naudialorraine.com

My favorite part of each day is the time I spend with Jesus. Learning and reading his word has transformed my life in so many amazing ways, and for that, I am truly blessed. As a graphic designer, coloring enthusiast, and all-around creative, I figured out the perfect way to combine two of my loves—Jesus & coloring was by creating this journal. I hope you enjoy using My Prayer Journal as much as I enjoyed creating it.

xo, Naudia

WWW.NAUDIALORRAINE.COM

LORRAINE

MY

Prayer Journal

BELONGS TO

Sheila Diane Morris Watson
given to me 11-22-20 by Paula Joy

Let us not become weary in doing good, for at the proper time we will reap a harvest if we do not give up - 1 Corinthians 6:14

Lord, I Praise You

Each month challenge yourself to do one of the challenges below at least once every day. If you want to push yourself a little harder, try twice per day - in the am and pm.

My Challenge Tracker

Start date:........................ **My Prayer Challenge Tracker**

HABIT	1	2	3	4	5	6	7	8	9	10	11	12	13	14	15	16	17	18	19	20	21	22	23	24	25	26	27	28	29	30	31
AM																															
PM																															

Start date:........................ **My Bible Reading Challenge Tracker**

HABIT	1	2	3	4	5	6	7	8	9	10	11	12	13	14	15	16	17	18	19	20	21	22	23	24	25	26	27	28	29	30	31
AM																															
PM																															

Start date:........................ **My Praise Challenge Tracker**

HABIT	1	2	3	4	5	6	7	8	9	10	11	12	13	14	15	16	17	18	19	20	21	22	23	24	25	26	27	28	29	30	31
AM																															
PM																															

Date: ....

My Prayer Requests This Month

Family & Friends

-
-
-
-
-
-
-
-
-
-
-
-
-
-
-

Others

-
-
-
-
-
-
-
-
-
-
-
-
-
-
-

My Prayers Answered:

Lord, I Love You

Date: ....

My Daily Word

Lord, I thank you for...
1.
2.
3.
4.

Lord, I pray for...
1.
2.
3.
4.

Lord, teach me to...

Lord, today I feel...

Today's bible verse: ....

Notes/Highlights:

Reflection & application to my life:

What lesson did I learn about God:

Lord, I Love You

Date: ....

My Daily Word

Lord, I thank you for...
1.
2.
3.
4.

Lord, I pray for...
1.
2.
3.
4.

Lord, teach me to...

Lord, today I feel...

Today's bible verse: ....

Notes/Highlights:

Reflection & application to my life:

What lesson did I learn about God:

Lord, I Love You

Date: ....

My Daily Word

Lord, I thank you for...
1.
2.
3.
4.

Lord, I pray for...
1.
2.
3.
4.

Lord, teach me to...

Lord, today I feel...

Today's bible verse: ....

Notes/Highlights:

Reflection & application to my life:

What lesson did I learn about God:

Lord, I Love You

Date: ....

My Daily Word

Lord, I thank you for...
1.
2.
3.
4.

Lord, I pray for...
1.
2.
3.
4.

Lord, teach me to...

Lord, today I feel...

Today's bible verse: ....

Notes/Highlights:

Reflection & application to my life:

What lesson did I learn about God:

Lord, I Love You

Date: ....

My Daily Word

Lord, I thank you for...
1.
2.
3.
4.

Lord, I pray for...
1.
2.
3.
4.

Lord, teach me to...

Lord, today I feel...

Today's bible verse: ....

Notes/Highlights:

Reflection & application to my life:

What lesson did I learn about God:

Date: ....

My Daily Word

Lord, I thank you for...
1.
2.
3.
4.

Lord, I pray for...
1.
2.
3.
4.

Lord, teach me to...

Lord, today I feel...

Today's bible verse: ....

Notes/Highlights:

Reflection & application to my life:

What lesson did I learn about God:

Lord, I Love You

Date: ....

My Daily Word

Lord, I thank you for...
1.
2.
3.
4.

Lord, I pray for...
1.
2.
3.
4.

Lord, teach me to...

Lord, today I feel...

Today's bible verse: ....

Notes/Highlights:

Reflection & application to my life:

What lesson did I learn about God:

Lord, I Worship You

Date: ....

Speaker: .... Passage: ....

My Sermon Notes

Notes:

Quote that I like the most:

Short Reflection:

Prayer & Journal Prompts

I love & worship you
Please bless
I have gratitude & I'm thankful for

Thank you Lord
Please forgive me for
Please help me with

My Thoughts & Reflections

_____
_____
_____
_____
_____
_____
_____
_____
_____
_____
_____
_____
_____
_____
_____
_____
_____
_____
_____
_____

Lord, I Love You

Date: ....

My Daily Word

Lord, I thank you for...
1.
2.
3.
4.

Lord, I pray for...
1.
2.
3.
4.

Lord, teach me to...

Lord, today I feel...

Today's bible verse: ....

Notes/Highlights:

Reflection & application to my life:

What lesson did I learn about God:

Lord, I Love You

Date: ....

My Daily Word

Lord, I thank you for...
1.
2.
3.
4.

Lord, I pray for...
1.
2.
3.
4.

Lord, teach me to...

Lord, today I feel...

Today's bible verse: ....

Notes/Highlights:

Reflection & application to my life:

What lesson did I learn about God:

Lord, I Love You

Date: ....

My Daily Word

Lord, I thank you for...
1.
2.
3.
4.

Lord, I pray for...
1.
2.
3.
4.

Lord, teach me to...

Lord, today I feel...

Today's bible verse: ....

Notes/Highlights:

Reflection & application to my life:

What lesson did I learn about God:

Lord, I Love You

Date: ....

My Daily Word

Lord, I thank you for...
1.
2.
3.
4.

Lord, I pray for...
1.
2.
3.
4.

Lord, teach me to...

Lord, today I feel...

Today's bible verse: ....

Notes/Highlights:

Reflection & application to my life:

What lesson did I learn about God:

Lord, I Love You

Date: ....

My Daily Word

Lord, I thank you for...
1.
2.
3.
4.

Lord, I pray for...
1.
2.
3.
4.

Lord, teach me to...

Lord, today I feel...

Today's bible verse: ....

Notes/Highlights:

Reflection & application to my life:

What lesson did I learn about God:

Lord, I Love You

Date: ....

My Daily Word

Lord, I thank you for...
1.
2.
3.
4.

Lord, I pray for...
1.
2.
3.
4.

Lord, teach me to...

Lord, today I feel...

Today's bible verse: ....

Notes/Highlights:

Reflection & application to my life:

What lesson did I learn about God:

Lord, I Love You

Date: ....

My Daily Word

Lord, I thank you for...
1.
2.
3.
4.

Lord, I pray for...
1.
2.
3.
4.

Lord, teach me to...

Lord, today I feel...

Today's bible verse: ....

Notes/Highlights:

Reflection & application to my life:

What lesson did I learn about God:

Lord, I Worship You

Date: ....

Speaker: .... Passage: ....

My Sermon Notes

Notes:

Quote that I like the most:

Short Reflection:

Prayer & Journal Prompts

I love & worship you
Please bless
I have gratitude & I'm thankful for

Thank you Lord
Please forgive me for
Please help me with

My Thoughts & Reflections

_____
_____
_____
_____
_____
_____
_____
_____
_____
_____
_____
_____
_____
_____
_____
_____
_____
_____
_____
_____
_____
_____

Lord, I Love You

Date: ....

My Daily Word

Lord, I thank you for...
1.
2.
3.
4.

Lord, I pray for...
1.
2.
3.
4.

Lord, teach me to...

Lord, today I feel...

Today's bible verse: ....

Notes/Highlights:

Reflection & application to my life:

What lesson did I learn about God:

Lord, I Love You

Date: ....

My Daily Word

Lord, I thank you for...
1.
2.
3.
4.

Lord, I pray for...
1.
2.
3.
4.

Lord, teach me to...

Lord, today I feel...

Today's bible verse: ....

Notes/Highlights:

Reflection & application to my life:

What lesson did I learn about God:

Lord, I Love You

Date: ....

My Daily Word

Lord, I thank you for...
1.
2.
3.
4.

Lord, I pray for...
1.
2.
3.
4.

Lord, teach me to...

Lord, today I feel...

Today's bible verse: ....

Notes/Highlights:

Reflection & application to my life:

What lesson did I learn about God:

Lord, I Love You

Date: ....

My Daily Word

Lord, I thank you for...

1.
2.
3.
4.

Lord, I pray for...

1.
2.
3.
4.

Lord, teach me to...

Lord, today I feel...

Today's bible verse: ....

Notes/Highlights:

Reflection & application to my life:

What lesson did I learn about God:

Lord, I Love You

Date: ....

My Daily Word

Lord, I thank you for...
1.
2.
3.
4.

Lord, I pray for...
1.
2.
3.
4.

Lord, teach me to...

Lord, today I feel...

Today's bible verse: ....

Notes/Highlights:

Reflection & application to my life:

What lesson did I learn about God:

Lord, I Love You

Date: ....

My Daily Word

Lord, I thank you for...
1.
2.
3.
4.

Lord, I pray for...
1.
2.
3.
4.

Lord, teach me to...

Lord, today I feel...

Today's bible verse: ....

Notes/Highlights:

Reflection & application to my life:

What lesson did I learn about God:

Lord, I Love You

Date: ....

My Daily Word

Lord, I thank you for...
1.
2.
3.
4.

Lord, I pray for...
1.
2.
3.
4.

Lord, teach me to...

Lord, today I feel...

Today's bible verse: ....

Notes/Highlights:

Reflection & application to my life:

What lesson did I learn about God:

Lord, I Worship You

Date: ....

Speaker: .... Passage: ....

My Sermon Notes

Notes:

Quote that I like the most:

Short Reflection:

Prayer & Journal Prompts

I love & worship you
Please bless
I have gratitude & I'm thankful for

Thank you Lord
Please forgive me for
Please help me with

My Thoughts & Reflections

_____
_____
_____
_____
_____
_____
_____
_____
_____
_____
_____
_____
_____
_____
_____
_____
_____
_____
_____
_____

Lord, I Love You

Date: ....

My Daily Word

Lord, I thank you for...
1.
2.
3.
4.

Lord, I pray for...
1.
2.
3.
4.

Lord, teach me to...

Lord, today I feel...

Today's bible verse: ....

Notes/Highlights:

Reflection & application to my life:

What lesson did I learn about God:

Lord, I Love You

Date: ....

My Daily Word

Lord, I thank you for...
1.
2.
3.
4.

Lord, I pray for...
1.
2.
3.
4.

Lord, teach me to...

Lord, today I feel...

Today's bible verse: ....

Notes/Highlights:

Reflection & application to my life:

What lesson did I learn about God:

Lord, I Love You

Date: ....

My Daily Word

Lord, I thank you for...
1.
2.
3.
4.

Lord, I pray for...
1.
2.
3.
4.

Lord, teach me to...

Lord, today I feel...

Today's bible verse: ....

Notes/Highlights:

Reflection & application to my life:

What lesson did I learn about God:

Lord, I Love You

Date: ....

My Daily Word

Lord, I thank you for...
1.
2.
3.
4.

Lord, I pray for...
1.
2.
3.
4.

Lord, teach me to...

Lord, today I feel...

Today's bible verse: ....

Notes/Highlights:

Reflection & application to my life:

What lesson did I learn about God:

Lord, I Love You

Date: ....

My Daily Word

Lord, I thank you for...
1.
2.
3.
4.

Lord, I pray for...
1.
2.
3.
4.

Lord, teach me to...

Lord, today I feel...

Today's bible verse: ....

Notes/Highlights:

Reflection & application to my life:

What lesson did I learn about God:

Lord, I Love You

Date: ....

My Daily Word

Lord, I thank you for...
1.
2.
3.
4.

Lord, I pray for...
1.
2.
3.
4.

Lord, teach me to...

Lord, today I feel...

Today's bible verse: ....

Notes/Highlights:

Reflection & application to my life:

What lesson did I learn about God:

Lord, I Love You

Date: ....

My Daily Word

Lord, I thank you for...
1.
2.
3.
4.

Lord, I pray for...
1.
2.
3.
4.

Lord, teach me to...

Lord, today I feel...

Today's bible verse: ....

Notes/Highlights:

Reflection & application to my life:

What lesson did I learn about God:

Lord, I Worship You

Date: ....

Speaker: .... Passage: ....

My Sermon Notes

Notes:

[ ]

Quote that I like the most:

[ ]

Short Reflection:

[ ]

Prayer & Journal Prompts

I love & worship you
Please bless
I have gratitude & I'm thankful for

Thank you Lord
Please forgive me for
Please help me with

My Thoughts & Reflections

___
___
___
___
___
___
___
___
___
___
___
___
___
___
___
___
___
___
___
___
___
___
___
___
___

Lord, I Love You

Date: ....

My Daily Word

Lord, I thank you for...

1.
2.
3.
4.

Lord, I pray for...

1.
2.
3.
4.

Lord, teach me to...

Lord, today I feel...

Today's bible verse: ....

Notes/Highlights:

Reflection & application to my life:

What lesson did I learn about God:

Lord, I Love You

Date: ....

My Daily Word

Lord, I thank you for...
1.
2.
3.
4.

Lord, I pray for...
1.
2.
3.
4.

Lord, teach me to...

Lord, today I feel...

Today's bible verse: ....

Notes/Highlights:

Reflection & application to my life:

What lesson did I learn about God:

Lord, I Love You

Date: ....

My Daily Word

Lord, I thank you for...

1.
2.
3.
4.

Lord, I pray for...

1.
2.
3.
4.

Lord, teach me to...

Lord, today I feel...

Today's bible verse: ....

Notes/Highlights:

Reflection & application to my life:

What lesson did I learn about God:

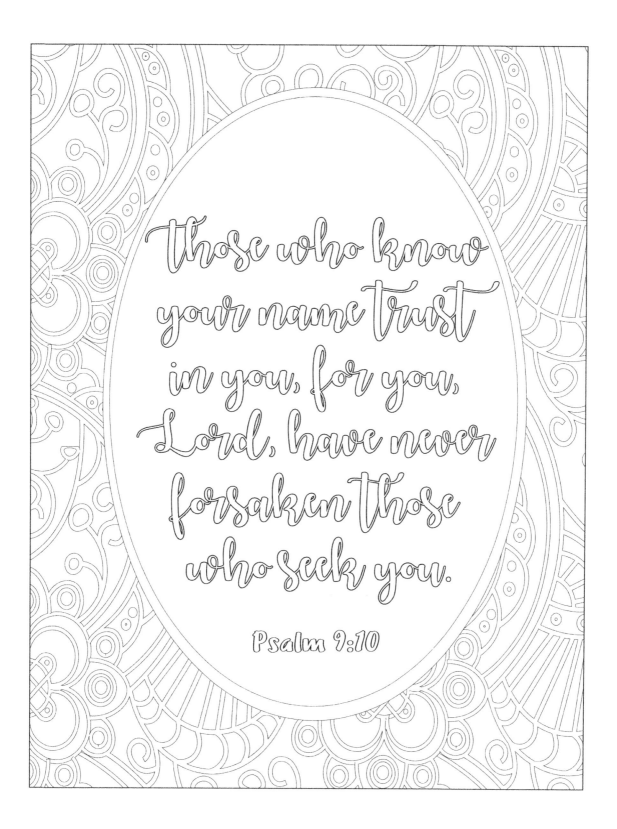

Lord, I Praise You

Each month challenge yourself to do one of the challenges below at least once every day. If you want to push yourself a little harder, do them twice per day in the am and pm.

My Challenge Tracker

Start date: ....

My Prayer Challenge Tracker

HABIT	1	2	3	4	5	6	7	8	9	10	11	12	13	14	15	16	17	18	19	20	21	22	23	24	25	26	27	28	29	30	31
AM																															
PM																															

Start date: ....

My Bible Reading Challenge Tracker

HABIT	1	2	3	4	5	6	7	8	9	10	11	12	13	14	15	16	17	18	19	20	21	22	23	24	25	26	27	28	29	30	31
AM																															
PM																															

Start date: ....

My Praise Challenge Tracker

HABIT	1	2	3	4	5	6	7	8	9	10	11	12	13	14	15	16	17	18	19	20	21	22	23	24	25	26	27	28	29	30	31
AM																															
PM																															

Date: ....

My Prayer Requests This Month

Family & Friends

-
-
-
-
-
-
-
-
-
-
-
-
-
-

Others

-
-
-
-
-
-
-
-
-
-
-
-
-
-

My Prayers Answered:

Lord, I Love You

Date: ....

My Daily Word

Lord, I thank you for...
1.
2.
3.
4.

Lord, I pray for...
1.
2.
3.
4.

Lord, teach me to...

Lord, today I feel...

Today's bible verse: ....

Notes/Highlights:

Reflection & application to my life:

What lesson did I learn about God:

Lord, I Love You

Date: ....

My Daily Word

Lord, I thank you for...
1.
2.
3.
4.

Lord, I pray for...
1.
2.
3.
4.

Lord, teach me to...

Lord, today I feel...

Today's bible verse: ....

Notes/Highlights:

Reflection & application to my life:

What lesson did I learn about God:

Date: ....

My Daily Word

Lord, I thank you for...

1.
2.
3.
4.

Lord, I pray for...

1.
2.
3.
4.

Lord, teach me to...

Lord, today I feel...

Today's bible verse: ....

Notes/Highlights:

Reflection & application to my life:

What lesson did I learn about God:

Lord, I Love You

Date: ....

My Daily Word

Lord, I thank you for...
1.
2.
3.
4.

Lord, I pray for...
1.
2.
3.
4.

Lord, teach me to...

Lord, today I feel...

Today's bible verse: ....

Notes/Highlights:

Reflection & application to my life:

What lesson did I learn about God:

Date: ....

Speaker: .... Passage: ....

My Sermon Notes

Notes:

Quote that I like the most:

Short Reflection:

Prayer & Journal Prompts

I love & worship you
Please bless
I have gratitude & I'm thankful for

Thank you Lord
Please forgive me for
Please help me with

My Thoughts & Reflections

_____
_____
_____
_____
_____
_____
_____
_____
_____
_____
_____
_____
_____
_____
_____
_____
_____
_____
_____
_____

Lord, I Love You

Date: ....

My Daily Word

Lord, I thank you for...
1.
2.
3.
4.

Lord, I pray for...
1.
2.
3.
4.

Lord, teach me to...

Lord, today I feel...

Today's bible verse: ....

Notes/Highlights:

Reflection & application to my life:

What lesson did I learn about God:

Lord, I Love You

Date: ....

My Daily Word

Lord, I thank you for...
1.
2.
3.
4.

Lord, I pray for...
1.
2.
3.
4.

Lord, teach me to...

Lord, today I feel...

Today's bible verse: ....

Notes/Highlights:

Reflection & application to my life:

What lesson did I learn about God:

Lord, I Love You

Date: ....

My Daily Word

Lord, I thank you for...
1.
2.
3.
4.

Lord, I pray for...
1.
2.
3.
4.

Lord, teach me to...

Lord, today I feel...

Today's bible verse: ....

Notes/Highlights:

Reflection & application to my life:

What lesson did I learn about God:

Lord, I Love You

Date: ....

My Daily Word

Lord, I thank you for...
1.
2.
3.
4.

Lord, I pray for...
1.
2.
3.
4.

Lord, teach me to...

Lord, today I feel...

Today's bible verse: ....

Notes/Highlights:

Reflection & application to my life:

What lesson did I learn about God:

Lord, I Love You

Date: ....

My Daily Word

Lord, I thank you for...
1.
2.
3.
4.

Lord, I pray for...
1.
2.
3.
4.

Lord, teach me to...

Lord, today I feel...

Today's bible verse: ....

Notes/Highlights:

Reflection & application to my life:

What lesson did I learn about God:

Lord, I Love You

Date: ....

My Daily Word

Lord, I thank you for...
1.
2.
3.
4.

Lord, I pray for...
1.
2.
3.
4.

Lord, teach me to...

Lord, today I feel...

Today's bible verse: ....

Notes/Highlights:

Reflection & application to my life:

What lesson did I learn about God:

Lord, I Love You

Date: ....

My Daily Word

Lord, I thank you for...

1.
2.
3.
4.

Lord, I pray for...

1.
2.
3.
4.

Lord, teach me to...

Lord, today I feel...

Today's bible verse: ....

Notes/Highlights:

Reflection & application to my life:

What lesson did I learn about God:

Lord, I Worship You

Date: ....

Speaker: .... Passage: ....

My Sermon Notes

Notes:

[ ]

Quote that I like the most:

[ ]

Short Reflection:

[ ]

Prayer & Journal Prompts

I love & worship you
Please bless
I have gratitude & I'm thankful for

Thank you Lord
Please forgive me for
Please help me with

My Thoughts & Reflections

_____
_____
_____
_____
_____
_____
_____
_____
_____
_____
_____
_____
_____
_____
_____
_____
_____
_____
_____

Lord, I Love You

Date: ....

My Daily Word

Lord, I thank you for...
1.
2.
3.
4.

Lord, I pray for...
1.
2.
3.
4.

Lord, teach me to...

Lord, today I feel...

Today's bible verse: ....

Notes/Highlights:

Reflection & application to my life:

What lesson did I learn about God:

Lord, I Love You

Date: ....

My Daily Word

Lord, I thank you for...
1.
2.
3.
4.

Lord, I pray for...
1.
2.
3.
4.

Lord, teach me to...

Lord, today I feel...

Today's bible verse: ....

Notes/Highlights:

Reflection & application to my life:

What lesson did I learn about God:

Lord, I Love You Date: ....

My Daily Word

Lord, I thank you for...
1.
2.
3.
4.

Lord, I pray for...
1.
2.
3.
4.

Lord, teach me to...

Lord, today I feel...

Today's bible verse: ....

Notes/Highlights:

Reflection & application to my life:

What lesson did I learn about God:

Lord, I Love You

Date: ....

My Daily Word

Lord, I thank you for...
1.
2.
3.
4.

Lord, I pray for...
1.
2.
3.
4.

Lord, teach me to...

Lord, today I feel...

Today's bible verse: ....

Notes/Highlights:

Reflection & application to my life:

What lesson did I learn about God:

Lord, I Love You

Date: ....

My Daily Word

Lord, I thank you for...
1.
2.
3.
4.

Lord, I pray for...
1.
2.
3.
4.

Lord, teach me to...

Lord, today I feel...

Today's bible verse: ....

Notes/Highlights:

Reflection & application to my life:

What lesson did I learn about God:

Lord, I Love You

Date: ....

My Daily Word

Lord, I thank you for...
1.
2.
3.
4.

Lord, I pray for...
1.
2.
3.
4.

Lord, teach me to...

Lord, today I feel...

Today's bible verse: ....

Notes/Highlights:

Reflection & application to my life:

What lesson did I learn about God:

Lord, I Love You

Date: ....

My Daily Word

Lord, I thank you for...
1.
2.
3.
4.

Lord, I pray for...
1.
2.
3.
4.

Lord, teach me to...

Lord, today I feel...

Today's bible verse: ....

Notes/Highlights:

Reflection & application to my life:

What lesson did I learn about God:

Lord, I Worship You

Date: ....

Speaker: .... Passage: ....

My Sermon Notes

Notes:

Quote that I like the most:

Short Reflection:

Prayer & Journal Prompts

I love & worship you
Please bless
I have gratitude & I'm thankful for

Thank you Lord
Please forgive me for
Please help me with

My Thoughts & Reflections

_____
_____
_____
_____
_____
_____
_____
_____
_____
_____
_____
_____
_____
_____
_____
_____
_____
_____
_____
_____
_____

Lord, I Love You

Date: ....

My Daily Word

Lord, I thank you for...
1.
2.
3.
4.

Lord, I pray for...
1.
2.
3.
4.

Lord, teach me to...

Lord, today I feel...

Today's bible verse: ....

Notes/Highlights:

Reflection & application to my life:

What lesson did I learn about God:

Lord, I Love You

Date: ....

My Daily Word

Lord, I thank you for...
1.
2.
3.
4.

Lord, I pray for...
1.
2.
3.
4.

Lord, teach me to...

Lord, today I feel...

Today's bible verse: ....

Notes/Highlights:

Reflection & application to my life:

What lesson did I learn about God:

Lord, I Love You

Date: ....

My Daily Word

Lord, I thank you for...
1.
2.
3.
4.

Lord, I pray for...
1.
2.
3.
4.

Lord, teach me to...

Lord, today I feel...

Today's bible verse: ....

Notes/Highlights:

Reflection & application to my life:

What lesson did I learn about God:

Lord, I Love You

Date: ....

My Daily Word

Lord, I thank you for...
1.
2.
3.
4.

Lord, I pray for...
1.
2.
3.
4.

Lord, teach me to...

Lord, today I feel...

Today's bible verse: ....

Notes/Highlights:

Reflection & application to my life:

What lesson did I learn about God:

Lord, I Love You

Date: ....

My Daily Word

Lord, I thank you for...
1.
2.
3.
4.

Lord, I pray for...
1.
2.
3.
4.

Lord, teach me to...

Lord, today I feel...

Today's bible verse: ....

Notes/Highlights:

Reflection & application to my life:

What lesson did I learn about God:

Lord, I Love You

Date: ....

My Daily Word

Lord, I thank you for...
1.
2.
3.
4.

Lord, I pray for...
1.
2.
3.
4.

Lord, teach me to...

Lord, today I feel...

Today's bible verse: ....

Notes/Highlights:

Reflection & application to my life:

What lesson did I learn about God:

Lord, I Love You

Date: ....

My Daily Word

Lord, I thank you for...
1.
2.
3.
4.

Lord, I pray for...
1.
2.
3.
4.

Lord, teach me to...

Lord, today I feel...

Today's bible verse: ....

Notes/Highlights:

Reflection & application to my life:

What lesson did I learn about God:

Lord, I Worship You

Date: ....

Speaker: .... Passage: ....

My Sermon Notes

Notes:

Quote that I like the most:

Short Reflection:

Prayer & Journal Prompts

I love & worship you
Please bless
I have gratitude & I'm thankful for

Thank you Lord
Please forgive me for
Please help me with

My Thoughts & Reflections

_____
_____
_____
_____
_____
_____
_____
_____
_____
_____
_____
_____
_____
_____
_____
_____
_____
_____
_____
_____

Lord, I Love You

Date: ....

My Daily Word

Lord, I thank you for...
1.
2.
3.
4.

Lord, I pray for...
1.
2.
3.
4.

Lord, teach me to...

Lord, today I feel...

Today's bible verse: ....

Notes/Highlights:

Reflection & application to my life:

What lesson did I learn about God:

Lord, I Love You

Date: ....

My Daily Word

Lord, I thank you for...
1.
2.
3.
4.

Lord, I pray for...
1.
2.
3.
4.

Lord, teach me to...

Lord, today I feel...

Today's bible verse: ....

Notes/Highlights:

Reflection & application to my life:

What lesson did I learn about God:

Lord, I Love You

Date: ....

My Daily Word

Lord, I thank you for...
1.
2.
3.
4.

Lord, I pray for...
1.
2.
3.
4.

Lord, teach me to...

Lord, today I feel...

Today's bible verse: ....

Notes/Highlights:

Reflection & application to my life:

What lesson did I learn about God:

Lord, I Love You

Date: ....

My Daily Word

Lord, I thank you for...
1.
2.
3.
4.

Lord, I pray for...
1.
2.
3.
4.

Lord, teach me to...

Lord, today I feel...

Today's bible verse: ....

Notes/Highlights:

Reflection & application to my life:

What lesson did I learn about God:

Lord, I Love You

Date: ....

My Daily Word

Lord, I thank you for...
1.
2.
3.
4.

Lord, I pray for...
1.
2.
3.
4.

Lord, teach me to...

Lord, today I feel...

Today's bible verse: ....

Notes/Highlights:

Reflection & application to my life:

What lesson did I learn about God:

Lord, I Love You

Date: ....

My Daily Word

Lord, I thank you for...
1.
2.
3.
4.

Lord, I pray for...
1.
2.
3.
4.

Lord, teach me to...

Lord, today I feel...

Today's bible verse: ....

Notes/Highlights:

Reflection & application to my life:

What lesson did I learn about God:

Lord, I Love You

Date: ....

My Daily Word

Lord, I thank you for...
1.
2.
3.
4.

Lord, I pray for...
1.
2.
3.
4.

Lord, teach me to...

Lord, today I feel...

Today's bible verse: ....

Notes/Highlights:

Reflection & application to my life:

What lesson did I learn about God:

Lord, I Worship You

Date: ....

Speaker: .... Passage: ....

My Sermon Notes

Notes:

Quote that I like the most:

Short Reflection:

Prayer & Journal Prompts

I love & worship you
Please bless
I have gratitude & I'm thankful for

Thank you Lord
Please forgive me for
Please help me with

My Thoughts & Reflections

Each month challenge yourself to do one of the challenges below at least once every day. If you want to push yourself a little harder, do them twice per day in the am and pm.

My Challenge Tracker

Start date:..................... My Prayer Challenge Tracker

HABIT	1	2	3	4	5	6	7	8	9	10	11	12	13	14	15	16	17	18	19	20	21	22	23	24	25	26	27	28	29	30	31
AM																															
PM																															

Start date:..................... My Bible Reading Challenge Tracker

HABIT	1	2	3	4	5	6	7	8	9	10	11	12	13	14	15	16	17	18	19	20	21	22	23	24	25	26	27	28	29	30	31
AM																															
PM																															

Start date:..................... My Praise Challenge Tracker

HABIT	1	2	3	4	5	6	7	8	9	10	11	12	13	14	15	16	17	18	19	20	21	22	23	24	25	26	27	28	29	30	31
AM																															
PM																															

Date: ....

My Prayer Requests This Month

Family & Friends

-
-
-
-
-
-
-
-
-
-
-
-
-
-
-

Others

-
-
-
-
-
-
-
-
-
-
-
-
-
-
-

My Prayers Answered:

Lord, I Love You

Date: ....

My Daily Word

Lord, I thank you for...
1.
2.
3.
4.

Lord, I pray for...
1.
2.
3.
4.

Lord, teach me to...

Lord, today I feel...

Today's bible verse: ....

Notes/Highlights:

Reflection & application to my life:

What lesson did I learn about God:

Lord, I Love You

Date: ....

My Daily Word

Lord, I thank you for...
1.
2.
3.
4.

Lord, I pray for...
1.
2.
3.
4.

Lord, teach me to...

Lord, today I feel...

Today's bible verse: ....

Notes/Highlights:

Reflection & application to my life:

What lesson did I learn about God:

Lord, I Love You

Date: ....

My Daily Word

Lord, I thank you for...
1.
2.
3.
4.

Lord, I pray for...
1.
2.
3.
4.

Lord, teach me to...

Lord, today I feel...

Today's bible verse: ....

Notes/Highlights:

Reflection & application to my life:

What lesson did I learn about God:

Lord, I Love You

Date: ....

My Daily Word

Lord, I thank you for...
1.
2.
3.
4.

Lord, I pray for...
1.
2.
3.
4.

Lord, teach me to...

Lord, today I feel...

Today's bible verse: ....

Notes/Highlights:

Reflection & application to my life:

What lesson did I learn about God:

Lord, I Love You

Date: ....

My Daily Word

Lord, I thank you for...
1.
2.
3.
4.

Lord, I pray for...
1.
2.
3.
4.

Lord, teach me to...

Lord, today I feel...

Today's bible verse: ....

Notes/Highlights:

Reflection & application to my life:

What lesson did I learn about God:

Lord, I Love You

Date: ....

My Daily Word

Lord, I thank you for...
1.
2.
3.
4.

Lord, I pray for...
1.
2.
3.
4.

Lord, teach me to...

Lord, today I feel...

Today's bible verse: ....

Notes/Highlights:

Reflection & application to my life:

What lesson did I learn about God:

Lord, I Love You

Date: ....

My Daily Word

Lord, I thank you for...

1.
2.
3.
4.

Lord, I pray for...

1.
2.
3.
4.

Lord, teach me to...

Lord, today I feel...

Today's bible verse: ....

Notes/Highlights:

Reflection & application to my life:

What lesson did I learn about God:

Lord, I Worship You

Date: ....

Speaker: .... Passage: ....

My Sermon Notes

Notes:

Quote that I like the most:

Short Reflection:

Prayer & Journal Prompts

I love & worship you
Please bless
I have gratitude & I'm thankful for

Thank you Lord
Please forgive me for
Please help me with

My Thoughts & Reflections

Lord, I Love You

Date: ....

My Daily Word

Lord, I thank you for...

1.
2.
3.
4.

Lord, I pray for...

1.
2.
3.
4.

Lord, teach me to...

Lord, today I feel...

Today's bible verse: ....

Notes/Highlights:

Reflection & application to my life:

What lesson did I learn about God:

Lord, I Love You

Date: ....

My Daily Word

Lord, I thank you for...
1.
2.
3.
4.

Lord, I pray for...
1.
2.
3.
4.

Lord, teach me to...

Lord, today I feel...

Today's bible verse: ....

Notes/Highlights:

Reflection & application to my life:

What lesson did I learn about God:

**Lord, I Love You**

Date: ....

My Daily Word

Lord, I thank you for...
1.
2.
3.
4.

Lord, I pray for...
1.
2.
3.
4.

Lord, teach me to...

Lord, today I feel...

Today's bible verse: ....

Notes/Highlights:

Reflection & application to my life:

What lesson did I learn about God:

Lord, I Love You

Date: ....

My Daily Word

Lord, I thank you for...

1.
2.
3.
4.

Lord, I pray for...

1.
2.
3.
4.

Lord, teach me to...

Lord, today I feel...

Today's bible verse: ....

Notes/Highlights:

Reflection & application to my life:

What lesson did I learn about God:

Lord, I Love You

Date: ....

My Daily Word

Lord, I thank you for...
1.
2.
3.
4.

Lord, I pray for...
1.
2.
3.
4.

Lord, teach me to...

Lord, today I feel...

Today's bible verse: ....

Notes/Highlights:

Reflection & application to my life:

What lesson did I learn about God:

Lord, I Love You

Date: ....

My Daily Word

Lord, I thank you for...
1.
2.
3.
4.

Lord, I pray for...
1.
2.
3.
4.

Lord, teach me to...

Lord, today I feel...

Today's bible verse: ....

Notes/Highlights:

Reflection & application to my life:

What lesson did I learn about God:

Lord, I Love You

Date: ....

My Daily Word

Lord, I thank you for...
1.
2.
3.
4.

Lord, I pray for...
1.
2.
3.
4.

Lord, teach me to...

Lord, today I feel...

Today's bible verse: ....

Notes/Highlights:

Reflection & application to my life:

What lesson did I learn about God:

Lord, I Worship You

Date: ....

Speaker: .... Passage: ....

My Sermon Notes

Notes:

Quote that I like the most:

Short Reflection:

Prayer & Journal Prompts

I love & worship you
Please bless
I have gratitude & I'm thankful for

Thank you Lord
Please forgive me for
Please help me with

My Thoughts & Reflections

Lord, I Honor You

Lord, I Love You

Date: ....

My Daily Word

Lord, I thank you for...
1.
2.
3.
4.

Lord, I pray for...
1.
2.
3.
4.

Lord, teach me to...

Lord, today I feel...

Today's bible verse: ....

Notes/Highlights:

Reflection & application to my life:

What lesson did I learn about God:

Lord, I Love You

Date: ....

My Daily Word

Lord, I thank you for...
1.
2.
3.
4.

Lord, I pray for...
1.
2.
3.
4.

Lord, teach me to...

Lord, today I feel...

Today's bible verse: ....

Notes/Highlights:

Reflection & application to my life:

What lesson did I learn about God:

Lord, I Love You

Date: ....

My Daily Word

Lord, I thank you for...
1.
2.
3.
4.

Lord, I pray for...
1.
2.
3.
4.

Lord, teach me to...

Lord, today I feel...

Today's bible verse: ....

Notes/Highlights:

Reflection & application to my life:

What lesson did I learn about God:

Lord, I Love You

Date: ....

My Daily Word

Lord, I thank you for...
1.
2.
3.
4.

Lord, I pray for...
1.
2.
3.
4.

Lord, teach me to...

Lord, today I feel...

Today's bible verse: ....

Notes/Highlights:

Reflection & application to my life:

What lesson did I learn about God:

Lord, I Love You

Date: ....

My Daily Word

Lord, I thank you for...
1.
2.
3.
4.

Lord, I pray for...
1.
2.
3.
4.

Lord, teach me to...

Lord, today I feel...

Today's bible verse: ....

Notes/Highlights:

Reflection & application to my life:

What lesson did I learn about God:

Lord, I Love You

Date: ....

My Daily Word

Lord, I thank you for...

1.
2.
3.
4.

Lord, I pray for...

1.
2.
3.
4.

Lord, teach me to...

Lord, today I feel...

Today's bible verse: ....

Notes/Highlights:

Reflection & application to my life:

What lesson did I learn about God:

Lord, I Love You

Date: ....

My Daily Word

Lord, I thank you for...
1.
2.
3.
4.

Lord, I pray for...
1.
2.
3.
4.

Lord, teach me to...

Lord, today I feel...

Today's bible verse: ....

Notes/Highlights:

Reflection & application to my life:

What lesson did I learn about God:

Lord, I Worship You

Date: ....

Speaker: .... Passage: ....

My Sermon Notes

Notes:

Quote that I like the most:

Short Reflection:

Prayer & Journal Prompts

I love & worship you
Please bless
I have gratitude & I'm thankful for

Thank you Lord
Please forgive me for
Please help me with

My Thoughts & Reflections

_____
_____
_____
_____
_____
_____
_____
_____
_____
_____
_____
_____
_____
_____
_____
_____
_____
_____
_____
_____
_____

Lord, I Love You

Date: ....

My Daily Word

Lord, I thank you for...
1.
2.
3.
4.

Lord, I pray for...
1.
2.
3.
4.

Lord, teach me to...

Lord, today I feel...

Today's bible verse: ....

Notes/Highlights:

Reflection & application to my life:

What lesson did I learn about God:

Lord, I Love You

Date: ....

My Daily Word

Lord, I thank you for...
1.
2.
3.
4.

Lord, I pray for...
1.
2.
3.
4.

Lord, teach me to...

Lord, today I feel...

Today's bible verse: ....

Notes/Highlights:

Reflection & application to my life:

What lesson did I learn about God:

Lord, I Love You

Date: ....

My Daily Word

Lord, I thank you for...
1.
2.
3.
4.

Lord, I pray for...
1.
2.
3.
4.

Lord, teach me to...

Lord, today I feel...

Today's bible verse: ....

Notes/Highlights:

Reflection & application to my life:

What lesson did I learn about God:

Lord, I Love You

Date: ....

My Daily Word

Lord, I thank you for...
1.
2.
3.
4.

Lord, I pray for...
1.
2.
3.
4.

Lord, teach me to...

Lord, today I feel...

Today's bible verse: ....

Notes/Highlights:

Reflection & application to my life:

What lesson did I learn about God:

Lord, I Love You

Date: ....

My Daily Word

Lord, I thank you for...
1.
2.
3.
4.

Lord, I pray for...
1.
2.
3.
4.

Lord, teach me to...

Lord, today I feel...

Today's bible verse: ....

Notes/Highlights:

Reflection & application to my life:

What lesson did I learn about God:

Lord, I Love You

Date: ....

My Daily Word

Lord, I thank you for...
1.
2.
3.
4.

Lord, I pray for...
1.
2.
3.
4.

Lord, teach me to...

Lord, today I feel...

Today's bible verse: ....

Notes/Highlights:

Reflection & application to my life:

What lesson did I learn about God:

Lord, I Love You

Date: ....

My Daily Word

Lord, I thank you for...
1.
2.
3.
4.

Lord, I pray for...
1.
2.
3.
4.

Lord, teach me to...

Lord, today I feel...

Today's bible verse: ....

Notes/Highlights:

Reflection & application to my life:

What lesson did I learn about God:

Lord, I Worship You

Date: ....

Speaker: .... Passage: ....

My Sermon Notes

Notes:

Quote that I like the most:

Short Reflection:

Prayer & Journal Prompts

I love & worship you
Please bless
I have gratitude & I'm thankful for

Thank you Lord
Please forgive me for
Please help me with

My Thoughts & Reflections

_____
_____
_____
_____
_____
_____
_____
_____
_____
_____
_____
_____
_____
_____
_____
_____
_____
_____
_____
_____

Lord, I Love You

Date: ....

My Daily Word

Lord, I thank you for...
1.
2.
3.
4.

Lord, I pray for...
1.
2.
3.
4.

Lord, teach me to...

Lord, today I feel...

Today's bible verse: ....

Notes/Highlights:

Reflection & application to my life:

What lesson did I learn about God:

Lord, I Love You

Date: ....

My Daily Word

Lord, I thank you for...

1.
2.
3.
4.

Lord, I pray for...

1.
2.
3.
4.

Lord, teach me to...

Lord, today I feel...

Today's bible verse: ....

Notes/Highlights:

Reflection & application to my life:

What lesson did I learn about God:

Lord, I Love You

Date: ....

My Daily Word

Lord, I thank you for...
1.
2.
3.
4.

Lord, I pray for...
1.
2.
3.
4.

Lord, teach me to...

Lord, today I feel...

Today's bible verse: ....

Notes/Highlights:

Reflection & application to my life:

What lesson did I learn about God:

Lord, I Love You

Date: ....

My Daily Word

Lord, I thank you for...
1.
2.
3.
4.

Lord, I pray for...
1.
2.
3.
4.

Lord, teach me to...

Lord, today I feel...

Today's bible verse: ....

Notes/Highlights:

Reflection & application to my life:

What lesson did I learn about God:

Lord, I Love You

Date: ....

My Daily Word

Lord, I thank you for...
1.
2.
3.
4.

Lord, I pray for...
1.
2.
3.
4.

Lord, teach me to...

Lord, today I feel...

Today's bible verse: ....

Notes/Highlights:

Reflection & application to my life:

What lesson did I learn about God:

Lord, I Love You

Date: ....

My Daily Word

Lord, I thank you for...
1.
2.
3.
4.

Lord, I pray for...
1.
2.
3.
4.

Lord, teach me to...

Lord, today I feel...

Today's bible verse: ....

Notes/Highlights:

Reflection & application to my life:

What lesson did I learn about God:

Lord, I Love You

Date: ....

My Daily Word

Lord, I thank you for...
1.
2.
3.
4.

Lord, I pray for...
1.
2.
3.
4.

Lord, teach me to...

Lord, today I feel...

Today's bible verse: ....

Notes/Highlights:

Reflection & application to my life:

What lesson did I learn about God:

Lord, I Worship You

Date: ....

Speaker: ....   Passage: ....

My Sermon Notes

Notes:

Quote that I like the most:

Short Reflection:

Prayer & Journal Prompts

I love & worship you
Please bless
I have gratitude & I'm thankful for

Thank you Lord
Please forgive me for
Please help me with

My Thoughts & Reflections

naudialorraine.com

Made in the USA
Columbia, SC
19 November 2020